# THE UNMOVABLE ROSA PARKS

Thuo Books

I am Rosa. I was born on February 4, 1913, in Tuskegee, Alabama. My father was a builder and my mother was a teacher.

When I was very little, we moved in with my grandparents because my father was traveling for work and my mother was expecting my baby brother. They lived in a place called Pine Level.

My grandparents had once been enslaved people and I grew up hearing how badly my grandfather had been treated. He inspired me a lot as he stood up for himself and his family despite it not always being safe to do so.

While we were not enslaved people, we were not treated the same as the white children. I felt very strongly that life was not fair.

The schools for Black children and white children were very different and this showed how unfairly we were treated. The white children had a newly-built brick school with heating provided. They were able to attend school for nine months of the year, as they were not expected to work. Only the white children had a bus to take them to school; we had to walk. Some of these children were mean to us and threw trash at us from the bus window.

For us Black children, school was an old building that had to fit about 60 students in one room. There were no glass windows, just shutters, and the boys had to collect firewood, as we had to heat the building ourselves.

We could only go to school for five months of the year, as a lot of the Black families relied on sharecropping. Sharecroppers worked very hard on the plantation but were only allowed to keep a part of the crops they grew, with the rest given to the plantation owner.

It was not long before our school got closed down. We then had to walk further to the school my mother taught at, until I was old enough to go to Montgomery Industrial School. When this also shut down, I moved in with my Aunt Fannie so that I could attend a public junior high school.

I remember when her daughter and I were confronted by a white boy who didn't want us to pick berries. Whenever I stood up to the white children, I would get told off, this time by my aunt, as the grown ups were worried for our safety. I always thought that it was unfair that we were not meant to stand up for ourselves.

In December 1932, when I was 19 years old, I married Raymond Parks, who was a barber. We went to live in Montgomery.

I really admired Raymond's courage in standing up for what he believed to be right. Just like me, he felt the way we were treated differently to white people was unfair and we got involved in the fight against racism.

Life felt more segregated in the city of Montgomery than it had been in Pine Level, as there were many more things that could be separated.

Even the buses had different seating for white and Black people, with the front of the bus being reserved for white people. Some bus drivers made Black people go to the front of the bus to pay, then get off the bus and get in at the back door to sit or stand at the back of the bus. Sometimes, the bus drivers felt mean and would drive off after we'd paid for our tickets, before we could get in the back of the bus.

However, not everywhere was segregated. One of the first jobs I got, after completing my high school diploma, was as a seamstress at Maxwell Field, an Army Air Force base. The lack of segregation at the base felt right. It felt so wrong when I left the base and had to go home on segregated buses.

One day in 1943, I got on a bus and there were so many people crowded at the back of the bus that it was impossible to squeeze through. I went through the front of the bus to get to the back but that made the driver very angry. He was a menacing-looking man. He grabbed me by the sleeve to get me off his bus.

As I was leaving, I dropped my purse and sat on a 'Whites only' seat to lean down and get it. The driver got so angry that I decided that I would never ride on his bus again!

However, twelve years later, on December 1, 1955, I accidentally got on his bus when coming home from work. By the time I realized this, I had already paid, so I just went to the back of the bus and sat on the front row that Black people were allowed to sit on.

When we got to the Empire Theater and more people got on the bus, there was one white man still standing. In these circumstances, it was common for the driver to reallocate one of the 'Blacks allowed' rows of seats for white people and that's what he tried to do.

The man next to me and the two women across the aisle went to stand at the back of the bus but I just moved to the window seat, where I sat defiantly. I was not needing a seat because I was physically tired but because I was tired of giving in to injustice. I knew that, if nobody made a stand, nothing would ever change.

Two police officers came and I asked one of them why they pushed us around. He responded that he didn't know but that the law was the law. I was arrested and put in jail. Only when my bail was paid was I allowed to leave.

I was not the first Black person to refuse to give up their seat but the repercussions of my actions left a huge mark in history.

On December 5, 1955, the day of my trial, a Montgomery bus boycott happened in protest. Black people refused to ride on the buses and walked, took a cab, or car-shared instead.

The trial found me guilty of breaking the state law and I was fined $10 and $4 in court costs.

That evening, a meeting was held at Holt Street Baptist Church and Reverend Martin Luther King Jr., a Baptist minister, was put in charge of continuing the boycott.

Life became very hard. However, just because things were so difficult didn't mean we gave up trying. After 381 days of boycotting the buses and many of us being arrested for being involved in the boycott, the Supreme Court said that the segregation on the Montgomery buses was unconstitutional. We were finally allowed to sit where we wanted to on the buses.

However, even though the Montgomery buses were no longer segregated, there was still a long way to go in fighting for Black people's civil rights.

For the rest of my life I did what I could, along with other civil rights activists like Martin Luther King Jr., to make Black people equal to white people under the law.

In 1964, the Civil Rights Act was passed, meaning nobody could be discriminated against due to what they looked like or where they were from.

For my bravery and dedication to civil rights, I received many awards and honors, including the Presidential Medal of Freedom and the Congressional Gold Medal. They even renamed 12th Street in Detroit to Rosa Parks Boulevard.

Over the course of her life, Mrs. Rosa Parks stood up for fairness, equality, and freedom for all. Her unwavering determination, love, and bravery touched the lives of everyone who knew her. In the last decade of her life, she was a Hero-in-Residence at the O Museum in the Mansion in Washington, D.C. as a guest of H.H. Leonards, who Rosa fondly called Lady H. It was during this time that Rosa met Pope John Paul II, was awarded the Congressional Gold Medal, was an honored guest at President Clinton's 1999 State of the Union Address, and even learned to swim at the age of 87.

A bronze statue of Rosa Parks stands tall in the National Statuary Hall of the United States Capitol, as the first full-length African American statue, showing her legacy lives on over 100 years after her birth.

To Mary & Martin, who were the inspiration for writing this book.

Written and designed by Lucy Thuo
Main Illustrations by Eryanto

Copyright © Lucy Thuo, 2025
All rights reserved.

No part of this book can be reproduced in any form or by written, electronic or mechanical, including photocopying, recording, or by any information retrieval system without written permission in writing by the author.

Published by Thuo Books

Although every precaution has been taken in the preparation of this book, the publisher and author assume no responsibility for errors or omissions. Neither is any liability assumed for damages resulting from the use of information contained herein.

ISBN: 978-1-917762-08-3

www.ingramcontent.com/pod-product-compliance
Lightning Source LLC
Chambersburg PA
CBHW041118070526
44584CB00002B/207